THE

POETRY NOW

BOOK OF POEMS

FOR PLEASURE

Edited by Kerrie Pateman

First published in Great Britain in 1995 by
POETRY NOW
1-2 Wainman Road, Woodston,
Peterborough, PE2 7BU

All Rights Reserved

HB ISBN 1 85731 600 2
SB ISBN 1 85731 605 3

FOREWORD

Although we are a nation of poetry writers we are accused of not reading poetry and not buying poetry books: after many years of listening to the incessant gripes of poetry publishers, I can only assume that the books they publish, in general, are books that most people do not want to read.

Poetry should not be obscure, introverted, and as cryptic as a crossword puzzle: it is the poet's duty to reach out and embrace the world.

The world owes the poet nothing and we should not be expected to dig and delve into a rambling discourse searching for some inner meaning.

The reason we write poetry (and almost all of us do) is because we want to communicate: an ideal; an idea; or a specific feeling. Poetry is as essential in communication, as a letter; a radio; a telephone, and the main criteria for selecting the poems in this anthology is very simple: they communicate.

Faced with hundreds of poems and a limited amount of space, the task of choosing the final poems was difficult and as editor one tries to be as detached as possible (quite often editors can become a barrier in the writer-reader exchange) acting as go between, making the connection, not censoring because of personal taste.

In this anthology over one hundred and fifty poems are presented to the reader for their enjoyment.

The poetry is written on all levels; the simple and the complex both having their own appeal.

The success of this collection, and all previous *Poetry Now* anthologies, relies on the fact that there are as many individual readers as there are writers, and in the diversity of styles and forms there really is something to please, excite, and hopefully, inspire everyone who reads the book.

CONTENTS

SEA SHORE

The call of the sea draws me near. My feet leave ghostly
imprints on the sand. I stand and gaze on the sea shore
wondering of distant lands and other sea shores. In my mind's
eye I see these lands far beyond our shores. I wonder anew at
the happiness there and want to touch it with my hands. The sea
draws nearer and I step back, my vision fades and I am back.
Back on my lonely sea shore lonely and forlorn.
I think of my vision of distant lands where happiness reigns and
no-one's sad. I wander the sands alone and sad wishing that I
could be part of that land. I sigh and look towards the skies, the
sun breaks through from behind the clouds. My heart lifts I'm
filled with joy. I realise I am but a boy.

Carol Arnall

AVALON

The stars fall down on Glastonbury Tor,
The moon lies waiting, waiting once more,
Waiting once more, for the light to shine on,
The truth that hides on this Avalon.

There old and frail, a man, by a lake.
'My lady', he cried, 'my lady awake'.
The waters lay silent, no voice had they found.
Drained of his strength he fell to the ground.

Then from his mirror reflecting the night,
The arm of his lady, clothed in samite,
Rose from the depths so dark and cold,
Her hand held firm a sword layered with gold.

The old man looked to the now rippling scene.
And touched the great sword for so much it did mean.
With his journey completed, he spoke of farewell,
His lady retreated to the dark distant hell.

I followed him close to a hilltop nearby,
Where the moon greets the earth that touches the sky.
From a cold silhouette to a warm burning light
He called to his maker to take him from sight

I returned to the lake where story books say
A knight cast a sword one cold winter's day.
Those winter days were here for so long,
But what of the knight who ruled Avalon.

Paul Bridgman

WESTERLY WINDS

Cliff-top walking
into the sun,
long loose hair
flowed
across my face
from right to left.
Turning land-wards,
the strands
ran at once
to meet the waves
of meadow grasses
and be etched into
the grain of that scene
where hedges leaned
eastwards,
prostrating themselves
to the Mecca of shelter.

Lorna Cooper

SCOTS PINE
(A Strong Image)

Ridged, scabbed,
Thick, impermeable,
Thrusting;
A lone giant,
Scarred like a furrowed face,
Unyielding;
A bastion,
Shouldering through
Scanty companions -
Unassailable.

Ann Burden

NAVIGATORS, WINDOWS
SCREENING LEANARDO'S

We'll all talk
　On the supernet highway
No pen or chalk
　Or Monday to Friday
We'll live in computers
　See what they do
Wonder of wonders
　Leave it to you
Global village
　Speaking on line
Have you a message
　Have you the time
Access infinity
　Endless the uses
Rent electricity
　Offer excuses
Curse the office, in house
　Learn rom, ram and byte
Look to see the desktop mouse
　Double speak in delight
Send all your wishes
　Respond see vous play
On airways and dishes
　Just give moderation a say

Chris Carter

AUTUMN AIR

Autumn air flows -
If you lift your head you can see fields
coloured by man's need -
Shot silk mist suspended above grass,
sparkling, morning-wet.

As the day warms, burdened fruit trees
and hedges stranded with blood bright
beads, light up, and freed by
the sun, insect gyros hover for final
nectar feasts.

If you lift your head you can see far fall
of land interrupted by firey woodland.

It shines, de-shrouded now.

The day plays its golden crescendo
all under a blue ark of sky.

Chris Rowley Langford

BUTTERFLY

To fly away on translucent wings
the wind the only barrier
To land a while and savour flowers
Then search to find another.
With life so short, there are no plans
and life is just to wander
Where it may lead counts for nought
'Tis the experiences that matter.

Chris Sherrard

THE STREAM

Towards the swirling stream,
I made my way to dream.
To sit on rocky shore,
And remember the past that is no more.

'Twas peaceful there that sunny morn,
The dew drops strike the break of dawn.
The ice cool chill of water fresh,
On pale white toes and gleaming flesh.

The birds they sang in morning choir,
And heron stooped in misty mire.
Kingfishers lay in wait of prey,
The sun rose higher to start the day.

I closed my eyes and began to slide,
In times before of which consciousness denied.
My first love . . . my only love,
Was cruelly taken . . . by him above.

The battlefields lay in pools of blood,
Bodies buried in sickly mud.
And there lay Charles, a dreaded wreck,
Shot through the heart as he fell to the deck.

The numbing silence was too much to bare,
The enemy retreated from waiting lair.
'At last!' his friends, they said they saw,
That by his death, they won the war.

As sun rose high and heat shone down,
I saw a man in silken gown.
Stretch forth a hand for me to hold,
A warrior in spirit, a body so cold.

As shadows lengthen to end the day,
A stumbling figure far away.
Grasped his heart as if to say . . .
Goodbye . . . my love . . . until another day.

Jane Cook

PRE-MARITAL CONTRACT

If you say you're going to make me your wife
I'll make you eat beans for the rest of your life
You'll cook me big breakfasts and always make lunch
If you don't comply you will get a big punch
You'll prepare Sunday roast and then pour out my wine
And set up the big table ready to dine
You'll pull out my chair before I take my seat
Then bring in the vegetables and carve up the meat
When we've eaten dessert you will go and wash up
Then make filter coffee and bring me a cup
You'll continue to spoil me throughout married life
That's what you'll get if you make me your wife!

J C L Smale

THE SALMON

The salmon wends her weary way
From ocean deeps to rivers play,
And forces up the waters torrent
Swirling eddies of muddy grey.

All around the perils mount
The men who fish and bears in wait,
Onward and upward does she struggle
In river shallows, to meet her fate.

The salmon migrate, their numbers large
Thousands of miles then to infuse,
New life to the species among the rocks
Though after this effort, lives will lose.

She deposits her burden in watery hollows
With eggs, which fish do prey,
But the salmon's reward is naught but death
Nature's betrayal at the end of day.

Steve Raymond

SISTER MOON

Sister Moon comes
sonorous and graceful.
Scattering her jingling silver
even in the dark places.

Bone-white fingers
probe night-leaves, tenderly,
and gently sweeping palms
caress shadows from the land.

Gerard Phillips

LITTLE BOYS

It's late in the morning and he is still not out of bed
I smooth his hair and touch his cheek, 'Wake up sleepyhead'.

He moves around hoping that I'll not see
'Come on sweety, do get up. Time for toast and tea.'

Washed and clean and breakfasted he gets up and says
'The boys are waiting now for me, I said with them I'd play.'

Out in a gang they kick a ball around
Then dirty and scratched comes to me, having fallen on the ground

I rub the hurt and hold his hand, trying to make it better
The problem is he's not my son, he's supposed to be my lover!

Kyra Lynch

A SUMMER MORNING

Crowning cock rouses the still slumbering dawn
Heralding in the rising of the sun
Who quickly drives the night dew from the lawn.

A sun beam trips across the bedroom floor
Gilding the sea shells gathered yesterday
On silvered sun-kissed sands and pebbled shore.

Sweet morning perfume wakes the drowsy bee
Luring him to flowers full pollen laden
Extracting from each one his golden fee.

Blackbirds breakfast on the window ledge
Under green watchful gaze of crouching cat
And birds strike up a chorus in the hedge.

Doors slam, loud footsteps clatter on their way
Down cobbled streets now filled with horse drawn carts
Morn takes her leave and welcomes in the day.

Joan Norman

FRIENDSHIP

Friendship, is being helpful
To people in need
Act like a boy scout
And doing a good deed

Friendship, for someone
When you know it will last
When talking of old times
And things of the past

Friendship, is someone
You think is a saint
Who's there unexpected
And helps you to paint

Friendships, are neighbours
You have near and far
Who give you a lift
When you need in their car

Friendship, is helping
Of those all alone
To brighten their day
With a ring on the phone

Friendship, is giving
Your seat on a bus
For somebody older
Without any fuss

Friendships, are made
By being aware
Happy and thoughtful
And having a care

Friendships, are something
You must find at all cost
Without it I'm certain
You will find yourself lost.

Frederick Arthur Boyle

THE SEA GREEN ROOM

The seas stretch further than the eye can see
Blues and greens are just here before me
Waves slowly crashing against the loom
Rushing together to form the green room

The room is what I see when I close my eyes
Rushing, crashing into the night skies
Deeper, deeper the colours submerge
Calming, calmer along the green verge

The green room covers the whole deep shore
Rage, rage the skies implore
Lapping along the solid straight pier
Catch me, catch me the sands leer

And so they chase the laughing waves
To the end of the pier, to the open caves
They jump and catch the crest marooned
And once again they are in the green room

Sian Ross

SNOWDROPS IN MUCH WENLOCK

And then the snowdrops came
Bringing you home to me
Arriving at my doorstop
Lost, sad, spinning non directional,

The snowdrops formed a sheet
As though to make our bed
And oh that we forbidden
Should lie together again

I plucked a snowdrop
And thought of our lost love
It seemed so white and bright
So full of hope as we were.

But snowdrops are a fleeting thing
It lived in my base
For just two days
Did your thoughts of renewing
and love last that long
I wonder?

Sue Hadley

CAMPANOLOGISTS

The melodic bells ring out their peal
Reverberating through this ancient tower,
Bell ringers restraining heartfelt zeal
Seem engulfed by the rhythmic power,
Keeping time as though in a trance
Like automata hands rise and fall,
All unaware of times advance
Dedicated ringers one and all,
Though it be twelve o'clock at night
When they are called to ring and toll,
Seen as privilege and not a right
Bell ringing is their chosen role.

Wilbar Ryson

SUPERMODEL

Perfect stuff gets strutted proud
As peacock, preened, unveiled,
Is tailed by eyes which never peer
Too deep, a funny game.

The cat walks, stalks, feathers fly
As huntsman in pursuit
Seeks quarry, takes aim and shoots.
Nice bird, exposed, takes cover.

Hung for a season, young flesh
Primed with care, prepared,
Plucked and dressed, made fit
For conspicuous consumption.

The bird looks blue. Jaded eyes
Drip tears as peacock in the rain
Peruses stately home. They say
Uncultivated peacocks have harems.

Sarah Turner

COLD MARCH MORNING

From this warm place
My eyes can go, still warm
Through cold glass, to colder still
The sheltered garden and its so
                                    familiar face.

From this warm place
Through snow and on beyond
To rest where sun at dawn
Sends light and shadows down to form
                                    this mossy lace.

From this warm place
Sharp sounds in chilly air
Darting movements catch my eye
Preened and feathered creatures
                                    excited by the chase.

From this warm place
The sun still climbing high
Dances on the waterfall
Which plunges deep and cold to
                                    end its final race.

From this warm place
I want to hold these moments
But they go on until tomorrow
To give their turn up graciously
                                    when new dawn shows her face.

Julia Fleming

SECRET GARDEN

Through the once-green door
now softly silvered, frost striated,
hothouses lean, drunkenly,
against flue-filled, sun-washed walls.
Vines, triumphant, rampant, tho' harvest lean,
vie with voluptuous, purple-fruited figs,
succulent leaves spreading finger-like shadows,
unmindful of human absence.
Espaliered peaches, medlars and quince -
untended, untasted,
too high for me to reach.
Cinder paths,
box-edged, rose arched,
lead from ornamental, exotic,
to English Apple-johns,
Bleinheim Orange, Beauty of Bath,
Adam's Pearmain, Pippins and Russets,
all queening the pillowy air
above the tangled, tussocky grass below.

Jane Pick

MOONKISS

How now? The orbs soft caress
Glides lovingly from soul to soul,
Naked to the eye and touch,
Breathes silently down your silvered flesh.
Bestow upon you, gently there,
As dreams unfold far inside,
Wrap you round without a thought
To give you all her tenderest care.

Children's eyes that gaze when closed,
Upon a realm of fairytale newly made;
In the folds of her ethereal gown
The budding nightmares are trapped and disposed -

And to child and man alike, should chance the bliss,
Of catching there, in the quiet hours
Opportunity to blanket your sleeping form
With the beauty of the moon's graceful kiss.

Paul B Whittaker

OLD AGE - SEPIA TONES

Everything in sepia tones
As the boat trickles to shore,
Not a sound except the water
And the rain, like drops in time.
As a photograph, it captures
This moment in stark reality;
A dreamy scene, you come to harbour
Safely to his refuge.
All around is sepia toned,
Framed by warmth and wisdom
Home at last with time to tell
Of sepia tones forever.

Diane Antoniazzi

THE LIST

A list ceases to be a list
Once it remains at home
When I've
        gone out.

Then it becomes tormentor in absentia
And each forgotten word
A blast
        of laughter
And a blank space on a dinner plate.

I stand here
        listless,
Dwarfed by a mountain of Co-op tins
High in colour and saturates
Me and my empty trolley
Overtaken in the fast lane
By those
        whose lists
                came here with them.

When I return home
With a basketful of guesses
I will find the cupboard
Already
        full of them
And on the table
Underneath a coffee cup
The
        Mocking
                List.

Judy Fairbairns

NATURE'S PAGEANTRY

The pleasant perfume of scented roses permeates the air,
butterflies with patterned wings, flutter by without a care.
Blooms of every hue are displayed - purples, pinks and reds;
the velvet touch of petals soft nestle quietly in uniformed beds.

Sunlight filters through rustling trees, whose branches lend their shade
to the beauty of a garden, deserving of accolade.
Summer parades her gown with grace, grassy cloak spilled o'er the land;
threaded with gossamer, silk, and lace-embroidered by angel's hand.

Yes, summer blesses with her delights, leaving memories to treasure;
Of a tapestry bright and colourful, bounteous without measure.

Christine Ann Morris

UNTITLED

Unassuming am I with regards superiority
but in some things that title suits me just

the other day
the gang said 'hey
let's go check out the spooky stone's roost'
and to that I replied that I would

a cold wind blowed
and their circle-oriented knowledge showed
I struggled too remain aloof
- and customarily subdued

but my mind was reeling
with answers, what a feeling
but a gulf remained between us

'it's the church on the hill - or was' I said
'it's historically proven, look . . . ' but no
because the info had a psychic source
and the facts were proven later
and to that it was I that produced this
the impact was sooo much lighter

in many ways I have tried to hint
from my psychically historical and truthfully high plinth
to all
not just this group of pals
but truth is for the seeker
. . . I said it's for the seeker

and now the job is left for me
and in the green and in print I'll presently be
witch eye new eye wood, seeee
after the dream of the golden beeee.

Brian Hoggard

SHARING

I peel the orange and carefully tear
the pulp into more or less equal halves.
And most times remember to leave
the toothpaste uncovered.
And when rising tiptoe about the flat.
For someone is there,
Asleep and about to yawn and rise.
I have someone to love,
To fight with and laugh afterwards.
Someone to share
The daily driftings, afternoon tea;
The rare delight of the world's approval,
The pain of its rejection.
The sadness of mourning,
Breakfast and dinner, a bed;
The beginnings and endings of journeys,
Projects, dinner parties, sunsets;
The uncertainties in moving to another place
With different smells, sounds, neighbours;
The angst and pride of children;
The going to, the being there,
And the coming home from a strange evening;
A cold.

Lawrence Holofcener

DAY DREAMS

It is dreams that keeps us going
Through the dark days of our lives
They bring us rays of sunshine
That brightens up grey skies.

To look out of a window
On a cold and windswept day
And dream of sandy beaches
On an island far away.

And as you close your eyes
You feel the warm sun on your face
You're the only human being
Who has ever walked this place.

Or stand upon a mountain top
Breathe in that crystal air
It feels like you're in heaven
And no one knows you're there.

Don't let these flights of fantasy
Just simply fade and die
They are dreams that keeps us going
They belong to you and I.

Val Thompson

NOT QUITE THE SUNNY SIDE

In the corner of my room I see
the sun has been put there.
Shines yellow on the wall
like a buttercup under a chin.
Perhaps

It will rest for a while,
observing itself on the tree outside.
The sun doesn't get a pension;
It's too old to retire,
stuck

In its ways. It moves lazily
across my arm,
highlights my own ageing.
I stare at the sun.
'Everything dies,' I say,

You're too old for this job.'
The sun smiles sadly
and drags itself off the wall.
'I know' it says,
'But people keep voting for me.'

Sarah Mooney

ON A DERELICT RAILWAY STATION

No more bustle, timetable or milk churn clanking;
No trains, no whistle, wires silent.
Now, wind-swept platforms lie forlorn beside a
          weed-choked track;
Roofless, windowless waiting rooms gape open to the
          rain and snow;
Plaster crumbles, ironwork rusts - all is dereliction.
Snow flurries hide the past and the day is
          strangely silent -
Save for the bitter winter wind whining through
          swaying wires.
And forgotten poles stand stark against a cold sky.

Barbara A Hughes

THE GLEN

Listen . . . The silence enfolds
like a warm scarf on a winters day.
Shades of green, brown and gold fill
the eyes and raise the spirit skyward.

Underfoot, the mossy ground caresses
tired feet, movement is soft and gliding.

Sunlight rays peek through trees
like warm loving eyes.

Butterflies glide by, their grace and charm
brings smiles to tired faces.

Heather white and violet, like bright
fairies shyly peeking out from
roots of age old trees.

Here, memory of the crashing - groaning
World of bricks, pavement sweat
and toil recedes!

A place of peace, colours and oneness
with nature,

The Glen.

Evelyn Peoples

FRIENDS FOREVER

Ever hopeful as a child,
Filled with dreams and brand new schemes,
Friends forever, so it seemed,
As together we searched, each to be free,
The urge to roam, to dance, to fly,
To sail the seas and reach the sky,
The need to go, to see
A whole new person each to be,
Yet while I remained so close to home,
You chased your dreams, the world to roam,
Your restless spirit had to see,
This other person you had to be,
You found yourself anew - so grand,
Climbing mountains in a strange new land,
All so exciting, vast and free,
And all so far away from me,
Though in my mind with you I roam,
Ever mindful of my home,
With its pastel shades and Wedgwood skies,
And all the grandeur it belies,
As you catch your stars and make trips to Mars,
Even you must realise,
As you observe the gracious sunrise,
The things we share, the things we see,
Never again the same will be,
The world is changing and so are we,
We have matured, our hopes procured,
The landscape never quite the same,
But bright new dreams begin again,

Judie Mackenzie

A WALK IN DECEMBER

Orion, his belt star studded,
Stands bold over this northern shoreland that I love.
I walk amongst naked trees, down to the beach.
Smell of the sea.
Windless, the air sharp as my awakening senses.

Along grassy dunes and up over a ridge leading down to the shore.
Moon shines through a gap in the clouds.
Framed by the clouds, rainbow colours encircle its cold whiteness.
Stars skinkle majestically, reminding me of my smallness.

The resulting rush of humility swells me with pride,
. . . And I smile at the contradiction.

Caroline Swan

TOUCHING A LUCKY STAR IN GOA

There is a golden, shimmering light there
Over the deep, inviting sea
There is a magic in the air

Cows of chaos, mirrored gypsies of Rajasthan
Intermingle like juggling balls on the beach
Multi-coloured
Vital orange and red
Spreads across the evening sky

There is magic there

As unspoken spirits gather
Unto The Lucky Star

Were you there?

Tito's rocks with the sound of bodies
Dancing
Several shades of black
Old Monk and Coke down the throat
Many accents, nodding news of all-night
Anjuna Beach parties

Well, it's Christmas you know

And there is magic there
There is a move to touch
On that Indian shore

In the gentle kiss in the air
In the sunset light

There is a beauty there

Nora Doherty

FROSTBITE

I want to break the ice with you,
    the coldness that lies between,
    to chip away at the icicles
    that hang there like prison bars
    protecting you from me.
I want to warm us,
    defrost us,
    thaw us,
    until Jack Frost is dead.
And on the grave of the Big Freeze
    the epitaph will read:
    The frozen truth lies here in state
    no longer able to isolate.

Kate Higgins

CHEMISTRY

The phrase, the glance
The shape, the chance
And the chemistry was right.

The touch, the thrill
The thought, the will
When the chemistry was right.

The gift, new bought
The pain, not taught
When the chemistry seemed right.

John Aldred

LESSON IN LIFE

When all around there is dis-ease
Find balance in yourself
Don't let anything get you down
Your strength will be your wealth

When others seem to criticise
Or tell you that you're wrong
Don't let mere words wind you up
Stay calm, and you'll stay strong

Make time to be with yourself
Just watch the world go round
Slow the rhythm of your breath
That's how peace is found

Realise worrying does not help
But simply show concern
And as your stresses disappear
A lesson you will learn

The key to life you hold yourself
And only you can know
How easy life can really be
When wisdom starts to flow.

Peter Davis

A PICTURE ALIVE

Your colour is immense
Your design is powerful
Your canvas is skin
Your story tells a tale
Your meaning not always clear
Your beam of life bright
Your intensity commands attention
You're tender and loving
You're cruel and savage
You're dark and evil
You're flowers and fairies
You're goblins and skeletons
You're life and death
You're a portrait for a thousand words
You're a picture alive.

Aileen Kowal

SUNRISE-SUNSET

What really lies between sunrise and sunset
a cool morning air a warm evening's scent
an echo that calls my name
the beat of a bird's wings
a sound like a shell pressed to the ear
a tide hitting a shore I cannot see
a distant thunder beckoning me on
that takes me from my reverie?
I salute the salt and taste the taste
and a boat lapped by the ocean floats free

I see the sun rise and see the sun fall
the child in me remembers with a laugh the hue of joy
and the swan flies within me

cool morning's purity mixes with the warm evening scent
and the swan beat has caught me released me
to where what really lies between sunrise-sunset

Alan J Summers

DISILLUSION

It fell from the heavens all sparkling and bright,
Shining as moonbeams and rich with delight;
It lay in my hand so resplendent, sublime
And I dreamed t'would be mine in the fullness of time.
In days light with laughter when fresh morning dew
Slips down from a dawning of heavenly blue.
It showered me with stardust from morn until night,
Yet it slipped through my fingers I'd held it so tight.
It ripped through my heart and splashed into the stream,
And there t'will remain to the end of my dream.
It lays in the pool now so muddy and brown,
And the sparkle has gone as it sinks deeper down;
When oft in my dreams by the pool will I stand
Something sparkling and bright I may see in the sand.
Stay thee deep buried gem, for with tears I can cope,
Would I barter my world for a glimmer of hope?

Margaret Marsh

PLEASE DON'T SMOKE!

Don't smoke . . . Don't do it!
Don't put your lungs through it.
A giant leaf with nicotine,
The daftest thing there's ever been!
Dried and rolled and later sold.
Money lost . . . Count the cost?
Who'd go out with you anyway,
If you smell like an old ash tray?
Other people breathe your smoke,
Even babies . . . That's no joke!
It's so sad . . . It's so bad
You're a fool, if you don't act cool.
D'you want to be dead?
D'you hear what I said?
Don't smoke, please don't do it!

Morwenna Stamp (10)

DO YOU KNOW?

I always thought I knew you
And that you knew me too
But when you really think of it
There's no way this could be true
Who do we really know
Do you know yourself?
Take a look inside
You know there must be loads to know
But the more you try to look at this
The further it moves away
It blows your mind
But everybody's somebody
Somebody no-one knows
There are some lucky people
Who have come to know themselves
I wonder when that happens
If you know all there is to know

Laura Williams

SPRING CLEANING

After winter comes the spring,
With dusting, cleaning, that sort of thing.
I though it wise to tidy up,
So I got together a pile of stuff,
And from that pile I built a fire,
Hoping that it would inspire
My thoughts about beginnings new,
And suggest to me what I should do.
When suddenly I realised
That all those things I'd stacked so high
Were thoughts and dreams and memories,
Familiar places I had been
And I felt an aching sense of woe
For all the things I loved, and so
I whipped some matches from my pocket
And set the lot off like a rocket.
I returned there later in the day,
Feeling regret and emptiness, but as I say
Fresher, newer, clear inside,
Strangely, just as the embers died.

Duncan Snape

NEVER MIND

What shall we do tomorrow?
Shall we take the car to the seaside?
Well . . . we haven't got a car.

What shall we do in the summer?
Shall we go to the Costa Brava?
Well . . . we haven't much money.

What shall we do after supper?
Shall we read the travel brochures
And watch the flash cars on telly?

Well . . . we haven't got a car
And we haven't much money,
But it seems we have our dreams.

Norman Sinclair

HARLYN BAY

I lie on my back on the summer ground,
And see the tamarisk upside-down,
Its feathery leaves moving way up high,
Brushing the clouds in a clear blue sky.
Oh! how I wish that I could fly,
Like the sea birds hovering tamely by.

The storms have had their wintry way,
They have moved the sand into Harlyn Bay,
And the summer children will wonder why,
The rocks have gone and the pools nearby,
But there's plenty of sand for a good sand pie,
and the sea birds will hover tamely by.

The air is bracing, the air is clean,
And I sit and gaze at the soothing scene,
And my soul sighs deeply and I know why,
And the tamarisk leaves brush the May-time sky,
And the pink thrift covers the cliff top high,
And the sea birds hover tamely by.

Jean Elizabeth Lewis

MRS GREENSTOCK

Mrs Greenstock fusses
When I leave wet towels lying around
when I put my apple core on her sideboard
when I walk up her rickety stairs with outside shoes on
Her dumplings and her eggs
and her steam puddings
are never quite right
according to her
and after all these years she still can't quite remember
the number of days there are in December

Mrs Greenstock has a poodle
that has hair appointments
that pees on me first thing in the morning
and again last thing at night.
Once I even kicked it, which really wasn't right.

Mrs Greenstock doesn't think
she should take twelve pounds ninety three
for keeping me
fed and tidy
four days a week
and she stops now and then as she hoovers
and says to herself, 'Fours into twelve pounds ninety three?
How do they do it? - Don't ask me'.

Sally Jane Webster

UNTITLED

Strolling through the forest
In the stillness of the day
Listening, as trees rustle
Imagining what they say

The sadness of the day
The hopelessness of life
As we try to make our way
Through the trouble and the strife

The peace and calm and serenity
As we wander hand in hand
Is all we ever hoped for
In this dark and troubled land

Many roads may lead us
Each day we journey on
We cannot see the outcome
Of either right or wrong

The crumpling under foot
Of the leaves upon the ground
Breaks the tone of silence
Peace is what we've found.

Delia Spalding

A BABY IS LIKE A FLOWER

You start life like a seedling safe in your Mother's womb,
But it will be many months before you begin to bloom,
You'll grow oh so slowly like the seeds deep in the ground
And like them also, you'll never make a sound!

Like the bulbs which start to grow and feed from Mother earth
You take in nourishment in the womb and prepare yourself for birth,
Just like in the garden when the fresh green shoots appear,
After nine long months in darkness your time is drawing near!

Then suddenly you find yourself bathed in a shinning light,
And your Mother sheds a tear or two and murmurs with delight,
Like the gardener in his garden when the flowers bloom bright and gay
Your Mother knows that God is near on this, her wondrous day!

Roy Swain

THE ROSE

Decorated with sparkling beads,
The rose stands.
Queen of the morning.

Her reddened lips, full and loving.
The gardener caresses her, soft and caring,
But weary of the thorns which bleed him so.

Paul Howard

FULFILMENT

She took a walk
Along the shore
At early morning light
And what she found there
Reinforced the love
She felt for him.

The cool grey water resting calm,
She likened to herself,
Awaiting with serenity
The love she knew was hers.

And when at length
He came to her,
In form of fiery sun,
His healing rays enveloped her
And filled her senses,
Every one.

Then afterwards, she lay relaxed,
Her sated body spent,
Her mind suffused with warmth and light
Her very soul renewed.

Ursula Madden

WAITING FOR THE BUS

He stood at the bus stop, sturdy,
Straight and very still; his
unruly straw-coloured hair lifted
upwards from the crown; every bit
of two and a half years old, impish,
unflinching in his gaze, splendid in
the brightly coloured clothes of
today's children.

Suddenly, there burst from him a
child's uninhibited, unself-conscious
chuckle - a cascade of sound
sparkling and joyful; his face
mirrored his happiness.

He did not reveal the secret of his
joy but for a moment the world had
seemed transformed by the laughter
of a child.

Margaret Willoughby

JANUARY MORNING

Dawn from the East
Indigo drift from the West
Gulls calling in the North, their message
                       to the mourning sea.

Silence among the trees, where
Last year's rookery, black with moss
Heavy hangs on lichen orange by half-dead tree.

Burble of near-sleeping owl.
Stirring of brown leafed hedge
As his robin peaks out to take up war.

Clouds run faster now
Above the still calm earth,
Freeing the ice-blades of brown weed to wilt
                       against the warming breath.

As honking pheasants clatter
Their last song; perhaps?
Today will soon be born, and Man
Stomp again his noise upon the world.

R E Wells

TUBE

Hurry hurry on your way
Brown and white
Yellow and grey
Skirts to ankles
Pelmets brief
That one's short
Oh goodness grief
Turbans black
And boots that clump
Packers trudge
With massive hump.

Eyes of almond
Hair so blond
Tower of babel
Sari gold.
Piccadilly, mind the gap
Pass your ticket
Through the trap.

David Mowat

DAYS

She held me like an April morning,
Beneath the hum and boom,
Of the mistuned radio set.

Three days, nearly,
Sank slowly inside me,
completely. Oh the guilt.

She held me, Violent Red,
Beneath the hum, drone and boom,
Of the mistuned set.

Jon Hall

ALIVE

To have space, time to think,
To breathe, not to sink,
Freedom to express, thoughts
In our heads, not to fight
For our rights, but to think.

To become our own selves,
To be strong and survive
In this world where the minds
Become stamped into one.

To define and express what we
Think to be right and to
Sieve the alive from the dead.

To see every day as a blessing
And a chance to relive and begin
A new dance.

Joanna Huband

SCULPTURES

The otter's fur gleamed
as it played in the sun
with its tail held fast
by webbed feet having fun.

The heron proud poised
by the diamond edged water,
Salmon leaping for joy
seemed to join the otter

An otter in bronze
A memory shown
for his friend Gavin Maxwell,
the otter man to mourn

Around the world his otters
give pleasure now, so much
especially the notice
boldly saying
'Please touch'
He himself to wonder why
now he's known as
The Otter-man of Skye.

Beryl H Grant

TRUE STORY

The day was hot and the children were cross,
And the shopping was heavy to carry.
My shoes were tight, the sun was too bright
And the old dog, she wanted to tarry.
The shop had no fat or fish for the cat
And I could find nothing for lunch.
I felt full of woe, had a long way to go,
And I walked with a kind of a hunch.
Then all of a sudden, from out of the blue
came a voice that was gentle and sweet,
My dear please don't hurry, there's no need to worry,
Spare a moment to rest on this seat,
Let the kiddies run while you sit in the sun,
And hear them laugh as they play.
You'll feel better my dear and more full of cheer
Because it's a beautiful day.
The moral of this I cannot dismiss,
It will always be in my mind.
Self pity for me must never more be,
For the man on the seat was blind.

Joyce Raymond

SWEETNESS AND LIGHT

You are my sweetness and light
Sweetness for a sorry day
You take the aftertaste away
And lighten up a mood
Darkened by this life

You are my comfort and joy
Soft and warm and welcoming
Comfort when you croon to me
And smooth my brow and soothe me
From these aches and pains

And when you're sad
And tears line your eyes
I will do my best to be your joy
And blow those clouds away

I'd like to sing to you
Sing you to sleep
I will watch over you
Watch you breathing deep - my sweetness

Your face lights up and you glow
Lights up my life and I know
That nothing man could make
Could be like you

Fashioned by God's hand with loving care
He put the sweetness and the shine in you
And he is who I have to thank
For all you are to me
My sweetness and light

Laurie Heighway

WHO CARES?

Sit on silk
Or on dust,
Have the best
Or the rust,
Some have all
Others none,
But one day
The time will come,
When every one
Will have the same,
And those with silk
Be put to shame,
For every thing
It must be shared,
The time has come,
To show we care,
Peace to all
In every prayer,
You must know love
Is always there.

Joyce Eastwood

BUTTER ANGELS

Butter angels fill my senses
Rip through tangled veins
Turgid nymphets fog my mind
Tear through pulped thoughts
Dreams of wisdom
Disturbed by bending oaks
Warm wind caresses them
No one knows
No one sees
Butter angels everywhere

Jack Scoltock

ONE HOUR

There is an hour when my soul needs resting,
A time when I must be alone,
When all the talk and the chat and the pestering,
Are too much for my patience to bear,
When the cry of the mob is wearying,
And the pleas for attention too loud,
And the din of the telly is past bearing,
When I must get away from the crowd.

My mind leaves for the world of my wishes,
And I'm absorbed in the fantasies I dream,
Please don't ask me to tell my secrets,
For they have meaning only to me,
And if I should tell them to others,
Why then my mind would cease to be free.

All I ask is for one hour,
Just one hour away from the clamour,
Just one hour to be on my own,
And then back to the love and the loving,
I hope I always shall know.

N R Labdon

SECRETS AMONG THE TREES

Solid, sturdy the oak tree stands erect.
Sheltering all that quivers beneath it
Rain pattering on leaves limp and green.
Roots absorbing the glutinous sodden grit
Birds above, chirping harmoniously,
Providing the air with desire,
Life scattering in various directions,
Dancing to the cordial choir.

Shambling movement, the squirrel descends,
The fare found and hurriedly eaten
Racing the moment, scaling the bark,
Intensifying the speed and time is beaten,
Secretly the Jay cradles an acorn,
With intentions to feast on quite soon.
Stout wings open wide, shading below
Framed by the glow of the moon.

Jane Cook

SECRETS

Inwards, the vista converges to your window, reaching
Your very eye, and on to the depths of your mind,
Where, you declare the many secrets lie dormant; revealing
Their effect according to your mood-some bitter, some kind.

Are secrets worth the pain or joy of hiding away,
Does concern or hope suspend other thought or care?
Who sets the rules to the game of life we unwittingly play?
But ourselves - and fate's tricks tempered with love and fear.

Sometimes, a glimpse of sub-conscious long since cast,
Or perhaps to wander where memories are the only mark.
Are secrets jewels of the mind or ashes of the past?
Love all enfolding, or evil thought fettered in the dark?

In your mind world where all is possible, and may be acted out,
How could I ever know or sense what these mysteries are about?

Lawrence Marson

WARNING

Never marry a mummy's boy
You'll only live to rue it
What! Take on mummy's pride and joy?
You really mustn't do it

He'll want his shirts ironed in haste
But immaculate in fact
Your hot pot will be short on taste
That his mother's never lacked

He really will expect to be
Waited on hand and foot
From bedside early morning tea
To walking out his mutt

His mum will come and stay with you
And linger on at leisure
With eagle eye on all you do
And how you treat her treasure

So do take this advice from me
And marry an orphan lad
Whose mum left him when he was three
And he's only got a dad

D Steele

MORNING THOUGHTS

Where swifts and swallows dip and weave
Shrill crying to the morning sky
Where nestlings lie in many an eave
And unassuming insects fly
Where drifted scents of rose and pink
Fill all the senses with delight
Where mornings bright and shining eye
Disdains the cataract of night
Where weary cat from night time roof
On sombre paw returns to rest
Here I my morning vigil keep
Whilst upon distant shore you sleep
Think not that any day flows through
Without a morning thought for you.

Rita E M Hunter

CRYSTAL CLEAR

Spirals of pure dancing light,
They sparkle and shimmer when turned to the sun:
To gaze deep inside fills my heart with such joy,
Entwines with my mind in a healing respite.
Facets of gentle refractions and spaces,
They enter my thoughts with their gentle perfection.
To feel through my fingers their tingling communion,
Transports me in dreams to more heavenly places.
Moon drops of crystal-clear dew;
They shimmer, and answer the song of my soul.
To hold these small fragments of fragile creation,
Inspires me with God's love anew.

Helen Gladwell

LONELY DANCER

I was alone in the midst of the crowd
As a cork on a storm-tossed sea.
For there was romance for everyone
But never a girl with a heart for me.

I sat alone and I watched them dance
And jealously envied each happy pair
For life was theirs, whilst I was dead
With never a love for my heart to share

So I wandered away and out of the hall.
Away from the crowd and the noise at last.
And I talked to the moon, while my lonely heart
Thrilled at the thought of a love to come
- And wept for the one that's past.

Peter K Greaves

PRESTON MANOR - THE SCULLERY MAID

Her hands and knees upon the floor,
She works with all her might.
She dare not trespass through that door,
For she knows the servants' plight.
She wipes the sweat off her brow,
She inhales the dirt and dust.
She looks bedraggled; her life is foul.
But she has to earn a crust.
Every order she must obey,
Though her eyes are sunken and weary,
But her duties she mustn't betray
However monotonous and dreary.
Her fingers are rough and worn,
As each hour takes it's toll.
Her face is furrowed and forlorn
And smeared with the black of coal.
The good life she cannot expect,
Though her dreams have often allowed:
Her *betters* she is demanded to respect,
But why hasn't she been endowed?
The rags she wears are ripped and torn,
Her shoes are ten years old,
She wishes that she was not born
In a world where her life is sold.
The blade of wealth
Cuts her down to size.
She rarely thinks of herself:-
A slave until she dies!

Laura Hartwell

PEOPLE

People shouldn't be stepped on
They should have their say
They should be respected in
      Every single way
Just take a look around you
And you'll be surprised to see
Someone with a heartache
That shouldn't ought to be

It's ordinary people that makes
      This world go round
And some are so quiet
They don't even make a sound

So if you're feeling sad and blue
Just think there's someone
      Worse off than you
If you can chase those blues away
Try and keep a smile for every day
You'll soon feel better in every way

Maureen Ann Thompson

CHECK-IN

Watch the white-capped nightingales glide from door to door:
fixed-winged angels, coaxing courage from cowed souls.
Watch, as mute grey shapes are trundled to and fro
down anxious corridors.
Watch me, here, waiting to join them,
an acute nobody with misplaced passions.
Why rage? Why grief? Fear would be more fitting
to this place between waiting and trial,
before the uncertainty of courage
and the redness of red.

Worst was waiting.
In the before the mode was *fight*,
dimming fear.
From that distance
the waiting promised solace.
Now, in focus, only illusion.
For, here I lie. Frightened.
Cherishing the gentle hug,
the whisper 'See you.'
Fragments of fragile hope
fall from the moving bed. Spent petals.
Rolling the silent corridor
I watch the streaming ceiling stars until,
beyond the sterile doors,
they coalesce to one bright-shining sun.

Tony Harris

A LOVE SO TRUE

A meadow full of flowers
A stream rippling by
And up above
A blue, blue, sky
All these remind us
Of your love.

Like the flowers
Your love blossoms
And grows
With each passing year,
Like the stream
A ripple of laughter
At a private joke
Though between you
Not a word you spoke,
And some days
May seem a little blue
Together you see them through.

So now you know
Why the flowers
In the meadow
And the stream
Rippling by
And a blue, blue,
Sky
Remind us of you
And the love that
You share
That is so true.

J L Harper

INFINITE LOVE

I will not ask for the moon
or the stars, the sky, the sea,
I will not ask for gems
just say you will always love me.

I will not ask for roses
or a palace to live,
Just your love and affection
and mine I will give.

I will not ask for rainbows
or even a treasure chest,
Just say you will always love me
and I will do the rest.

I will not ask for silver
just a plain band of gold,
And that you will love me forever
to have and to hold;.

I will love you till the sea runs dry
or till the grass turns blue,
I will love you till the heavens fall
my love is all for you.

I will love you in the summer
and in the winter too,
I will love you all four seasons
my love for you is true.

I will love you till the end of time
or till the day I die,
But still I will go on loving you
up in the heavens high.

V J Beaman

MRS B (OR BARFOOT-ATTASINK)

Almonds, anchovies, antiques, ants;
How to launder the underpants.
Bunions, bath buns, buying a house,
The law regarding an errant spouse.

Venison, verrucae, vermicelli,
What to do for a pain in the belly.
Clearing away when the food's all eaten;
How would I survive without Mrs Beeton?

Sue Rea

ONE OF GOD'S CREATIONS

With muscles so strong and as tight as a drum
And feet like a cat's paw for speed as he runs.
Eyes that glow bright and as sharp as a hawks
And long, slender legs that prance as he walks.
Powerful jaws as strong as tough steel
Sharp razor teeth that can possibly kill.
His smooth-skinned body so supple and firm
Can fly like the wind and can twist and turn.
For to chase he must and to catch he tries
The fate of the hare unto him does it lie.
Alas it is sad that some creatures are bred
To chase and to kill till the ground stains with red.
But when he's at home and in gentle repose
With soft sloppy eyes and a wet sloppy nose.
To be sure there's no gentler creature you'll find
One of God's great creations it is a greyhound.

Julie Waight

TO MY DARLING MOTHER

Twilight days rushing by,
Friends departing, ever nigh,
Retiring late, make the most,
Rising early, catch the post.

Look to the future, not the past,
Loving memories, make them last,
Make the most of what is left,
Do not consider, the bereft.

Ever eager, try to be,
Everyone's Epiphany,
Never failing in endurance,
Remaining always, ever prudent.

You must accept that life goes on,
Opinion's free for everyone,
Generations one, two, three,
All these age groups must agree.

No good relying on providence,
Must learn from own experience,
Difficult, it seems to me,
To realise, that this could be.

Perhaps, if ever I get old,
No doubt, like you, I'll get told,
Let us learn from our mistakes,
Like bone china, easy breaks.

Gill Walker

NORFOLK OCTOBER

A pungent smell of woodsmoke
Rides the drowsy morning air.
Along the lane white scarves of mist
Caress the hedgerow's hair.
No ripple laps the languid lake
That nestles in the fold,
Its sylvan sentinels arrayed
In russet and in gold.

These fields, once yellow summer seas
Of undulating corn,
Now wear designer stubble, all
Their former glory shorn.
This rural scene of cattle, farm
And now quiescent land
Awaits the unforgiving touch
Of winter's icy hand.

A P Gallard

THE COUNTRYSIDE

The countryside looks lovely with its fields of green and gold,
The giant oak, its branches spread, so beautiful and old.
Buttercups and daisies, clover smelling sweet,
The lush green grass, so fresh and new, feels soft beneath my feet.

As I look across the meadow, where the sky joins with the land,
I know unless you've seen it, you will not understand.
The loveliness of meadows, all fresh with morning dew,
Sparkling in the morning sun, wonderful and new.

The golden glow of summer corn, reaching to the sky,
The whisper of a gentle breeze, just like a lover's sigh.
Tiny raindrops glisten just like diamonds in the sun,
You feel you have to gather them, each and every one.

I wander down a leafy lane and climb up on a hill,
Everything's so beautiful, so peaceful and so still.
Then far away across the land, I spied a silver stream,
It tinkled and sang as it flowed along, like music in a dream.

Tiny creatures rustle in the hedges and the grass,
The chirping of the little birds that wait for me to pass.
So lovely is the countryside, and the sky of pastel blue,
And if you come out walking I will share it all with you.

Dorothy Smith

THE LIFE WITHIN

The light of love shines from within her
Like bright beacons of humanity
The world is her child,
Nestling in the bosom of her soul

Fragile feelings encircle her heart
Ever a target for life's bitterness
Eternal optimism her only shield
Against cruel voices that echo in the dark

Such is the life within her
More bounteous than flesh and blood
The true essence of sweet nature's bloom
The gift of human love

Catherine Roddie

FOR VIOLET

To you of love I'd like to write,
If only I knew how,
But though I dream of you my dear,
Words seem to fail somehow,
Oh for the gift of writing words
Like some smart writer chap,
But I'm not there, my mind's a blank,
I feel a proper sap,
When I sit down with pen in hand
I wonder what to write
I sit there staring into space
I wonder if I'm right.
No words come tumbling from my pen
The paper lies unmarked
Oh, what a grievous thing it is
When the mind lies parked
Many thoughts they come and go
But nothing gets put down
My head goes round in circles
I'm feeling such a clown
But wait, what's this that's coming through
Three words, but they're not new,
Three words which do but tell it all
Just three words, I love you.

Jonty

LILY

We went there
And Lily was gone.
Her view of the world
Through aspidistra cloaked windows
In the green half light
Of a dry Sunday
In a damp persuasive room;
Where the bricks, hammered in
To make the floor
Were covered by carpet worn down
By visiting.
Childhood's children, now older,
Remember her, and the damp
That is only recalled on reflection;
Remember instead the sunlight dust
Through the door leading back,
And everlasting smells of buns and bacon.
And her view of the world, green,
Before they took it away,
Took it and shaped it into something
New, and undamp as a bank manager's eye;
Lived in not by love, but by design. then
They knocked it down (for a price),
And all the Lillies of the World
Went with it.

Letitia Hughes

THE BRIDGE STREET CALL

A quiet bridge on the River Test,
Full of wonder awe and beauty,
An *Olde Cottage* overlooks the dream
Of tranquil scenes so gently!

Moorhens, swans, coots, ducks alike!
Gather there in numbers?
Little pathways which they tread,
In awe inspiring curiosity,

Far away from modern bustle
Are their thoughts so full,
'Bread' they shout, 'Oh how wonderful!'
In scenes long gone today.

D J Evans

TIMES RETRACED

In the autumn gloom
of my small room
a soaring voice takes over:
From musty cover I discover,
suddenly, joy I can't define,
that wondrous early zest of mine.
Forgotten long these records old
and half my youth the tales they've told,
for what I chose long years gone by
was me, then; and now I sigh
for the me that was then:
The record plays over again and again
and the dreams return - and the love -
and the pain
but the love will remain.

Pamela Broster

SILENT LAUGHTER

The comic stands alone
His lines are fast and hot
With his prestidigi-what-not
Like a monarch on his throne:

The man who laughter makes
Is a champion of the hour
But subtlety and humour
Our mind, our world he shakes:

The comic stands apart
Long hair, or silent tongue
No injustice goes unsung
By the impact of his art:

Charlie Chaplin, Harpo Marx
Silent wonders make us gasp
This greatest truth we all must grasp
By humour of silent syntax -

When the meek do inherit the earth
The greatest of weapons - shall be mirth:

Daniel Murdoch

BIRTH OF A CHILD

The exhaustion is over and all the pain has gone.
The cry of your baby is a debutante song.
You first glance in wonder, a miracle you see;
Is it true that this little person is really part of me?

So proud - you're a parent, so full of wonder you cry
'Has it got ten fingers?' Is your first worried cry.
'Yes!' Is the answer, 'Thank God!' You reply.
You can then watch the nurses go scurrying by.

Your loved one beside you who through all the pain
Had so much to lose, yet so much to gain
Helped with your worries, your hand he held tight
Because deep down inside was frightened he might
Lose his most precious while giving life.
Oh, now just look, he's so proud of his wife!
Look to his face, look deep in his eyes
Because he's so proud, Crystal tears of surprise.

Margaret Bristow

IN THE WEEK THAT WAS IN 1994

He signalled me to stop.
I rolled the window down.
He asks me for identity.
Growing boy
disguised as man in uniform.
He handles my licence,
then hands it back to me.
He rolls his left hand
into his right hand.
Confessing,
'I'm cold and sleepy
standing here all night
looking after you people of Warrenpoint.'

Kathleen Carville

THE EVEREST OF EVERY MAN

Man has conquered Everest,
Hip, hip, hip hooray,
Though many have never been there,
It is conquered every day.

The struggle is long and painful,
Many journey there alone,
Treading ground that never before existed,
Another's footprints are unknown.

And the joy that wells inside you,
Having reached your Everest,
Is the joy that comes from knowing,
You are at your very best.

And sitting on the summit,
You may slip off now and then,
But strengthened by belief in self,
You get up and start again.

Pauline B Ogilvie

NEW LOVE

Bright were their eyes
With the first flush of love
So tender the kiss
On each others' lips

So gentle the touch
So smooth the caress
So meaning the words
The ones left unsaid

So peaceful the silence
The silence of love
When words are lost
In the rhythm of life.

R A Williams

THANK YOU!

Thank you for the moments
We've snatched alone together.
And for the memories
That will stay in my heart forever.

Thank you for the love
That only you and I can share.
For the satisfaction of knowing,
Someone out there really cares.

But most of all, *Thank you*,
For holding me in your arms,
Kissing and caressing me
With all your loving charms.

S Harris

REFLECTIONS ON SILVIA PLATH

Resting in your nettle grave,
Your purple soul weaves and entrances,
Like an enchanted cello caressed
By the nectar breath which whispers from your lips.

My living willow grave
Is animated by the colours and matter
Of your clear weeping wandering stream
Which flows breathing in my purple force: My blood.

Now you stroke my mind like a lover
And warm my chill core with your radiance,
Like a golden ray kisses a spring dew-drop,
Our being intertwine like ivy choking the terror tree.

My pen flows with your mid-summer frost,
As your wandering ends like the dead within us.

Nigel Pearce

THIS LETTER

Had I lent my ears once, twice, more often,
And let you have your say,
Had I smiled or frowned at the sweet sound,
I might not feel this way.

Had I tasted the salt stains on your cheeks.
That resulted from my deeds
Had I tried to be a better love,
And striven for your needs.

Your love was a precious gift accrued,
But alas, I could not keep the jewel,
Thieves came and stole it, late at night,
And left an empty case, my plight.

Your affection I did take for granted,
Never watered seeds that you had planted,
Now love songs make me cry and weep,
And shallow is my depth of sleep.

Oh I lament, what have I done?
For now you love another one,
You were a candle, shining bright,
But now cold darkness fills my night.

Had I been, where and when you needed me,
If I had behaved much better,
I would not be here, on my own,
I would not have this letter.

Rachael Culley

DRIFTING

Last night the sea roared
And I in my bed listened
And wondered,
Of a secret world
Beneath its angry crest.
I moved through its wonder
And felt no cold, nor pain for air.
Just an easiness of mind,
A distance
From all that was above.

Denise Arundell

LIMESTONE MAN

I loved your face and hands,
Cool graceful sculptures
Beautifully hewn.
Delighting in the springs of our emotions,
We revelled in their ebb and flow:-
Heedless of the caverns time wore
To your drowning heart.

J Craven

ODYSSEY

The old man stared long with brooding gaze
Then veined hand lifted the twisted cane
And with it, pointed thru' the dancing haze
Towards a distant rise in the terrain
Above and beyond the dusty olive trees
Behind, a glimpse of placid azure seas.

'There, that path' he said 'Take that until
You reach the remnants of a ruined place
And make your way around that stone capped hill
To stand where the sun full strikes your face
Across the valley you will sight the peak
Crowning the dark mountain that you seek'

He touched my arm 'Few others who have trod
That path, have found a lasting symmetry
It leads to Temenos, the precinct of a God
There dwells an ancient world divinity
Whatever you pursue, approach with care
Although, if anywhere, you'll find it there.'

I proffered thanks and moved along the road
Wondering as to the source of his belief.
Cautious to visit such devout abode
Yet somehow, lightened, conscious of relief
Perchance my journey's limit now was near
Although in truth, my purpose was unclear.

I'm travelling still, along that dusty track
Passing those olive trees of silver grey.
The sun strikes fiercely still upon my back
The weary pale green vines yet mark the way
But my heart quickens as the time goes past
Perhaps there, my own God I'll find at last.

P Slater

DAD'S SHOES

A pair of tattered cord shoes, laces careless,
Surrounded by carpet.
An island within walls.
The striped lining stands erect -
A rebuke
To the lax line of the languid tongue,
The undulation of the patient piping,
The upcurved sneer of the rubber edged toe.
                    The left shoe is slightly forward,
         The right coyly back.
Both point towards the heat source,
Airing their sneers.

Patricia Bullock

NIKKI JAYNE

Her hair is long and curly
and her eyes are wide and green
you'd love her if you knew her
'cause she really is a dream.
she has the sweetest nature
and she has the cutest smile.
she holds her head up very high
and carries it with style.

I'm standing in the doorway
and it's pouring down with rain
and like so many times before
I wait, for Nikki Jayne.
She's stood me up before you know
and she'll stand me up again
and yet I know I'll wait and wait
and wait, for Nikki Jayne.

We said we would meet for lunch today
and then we would go shopping
but the longer that I wait here
I think she has forgotten.

Well Nikki is my daughter
and she's nearly twenty two
she's beautiful, but then,
I think I'm prejudiced don't you?

Gaye Fox

THE SCHOOL TEAM

We stood out by ourselves
With no-one else to watch
The school had hand picked all of us
To play a football match.

With Puis McIntyre up in front
And Gavin Strunks behind
And Ciaran Leonard stood in goal
Our team was looking fine.

The ref he blew the whistle
The ball was put into play
Andrew Porter passed it back
And I kicked it away.

For the next ninety minutes
We ran ourselves to death
Brendan Gill was looking good
Eamon Donelly out of breath.

The match was nearly over
When Porter stuck it in
And harpo jumped up from the bench and yelled 'I
Knew we'd win.'

And when the final whistle came
William Miller clapped his hands
John Strunks' legs were tired
But we were a happy band.

Cahir Crossan (10)

PHARISAIC MINDS

It takes one voice
To make the choice,
Just how your life is run.
They make it sad when it should be fun
Always moaning about every thing
Why can't they see what life can bring,
Why do they make our lives miserable and sad
When all you want is to be happy and glad,
There's things you would like to say
But it never seems to be the right day.
You wish in your heart that they would see
Just the effect it's having on you and me,
Do they not care about what they say
The hurt and pain, they throw our way
The rudeness of their voice
Just goes to prove we have no choice.
We hope the day will finally come
Instead of abuse they will be struck dumb.

Maggie

OLD AGE

Old age comes to everyone,
No matter what the class,
Black and white it's all the same,
You know that youth has past.

Knobbly knees and creaky joints,
You put on a smile,
No matter how much you try,
You cannot walk with style.

We are told to accept it,
This old age fearsome thing,
Words fall false we cannot hear,
Prefer to have a fling.

Dr calls and says with a smile,
You're looking very fit,
He must be as old as me,
I think it's time he quit.

Meals on wheels all taste the same,
Come hot in a pack,
I try what may to eat this way,
Most of it goes to the cat.

The family call and say, oh gran,
You're looking nice, they say,
Your frock looks smart, you don't look old,
And really made my day.

When old age comes along,
Greet it with a smile,
You've had your day, so they say,
It's time to dream awhile.

Daisy Cooper

DEEP GAZE

Further afield this great life takes us
Defying limits we could ever foresee
When ideology forsakes us
And strands us in anonymity

Life's tapestry - the purest thread
Is woven 'round our deepest fears
A tiny trace of what's ahead
Contained in all those passing years

Are we forever exiled on foreign shores
With no control of destiny?
A servile creature on all fours
Wondering what our fate might be.

Charlie Maunsell

BOOK OF MEMORIES

When I want to see you,
I flick through the pages of my mind,
Memories forever printed,
Never to be lost in time.

Images pass before me,
I see your face so clear,
I open the book of memories,
To always have you near.

The book of memories will never age,
And you are there on every page,
To me you will never be gone,
Because of memories,
You live on.

Images pass before me,
I see your face so clear,
I open the book of memories,
To always have you near.

K Baiton

LATE ARRIVAL

Have you forgotten? A poor excuse
When the flower-shop reminds us
Each time we pass!
See there on the glass
The winged feet of the messenger of love
He carries that token of deep affection
A single rose
Do you suppose
I'm so preoccupied with other things
That I won't notice?

You said I was special. Not like the rest
Only the best for someone like me.
I smiled, looked away
But you'd just made my day.
Yet no bloom came to confirm that statement
Nor scent the air of my room.
'Miss Rea' asked the man
With the little red van.
He presses cellophane into my arms
I bury my face in a dozen red roses.

Rachel Rea

GOD'S CATHEDRAL

The sunlight slants through darkened trees,
Its dapples dance on whispered breeze,
The silence hangs on spider's web,
As God's cathedral steps I tread.

In reverence my eyes behold,
Tall oak trees formed in days of old,
Not by human hand long gone,
But fashioned by the ageless one.

No better windows could I view,
Than hawthorn blossom's fragrant hue,
The carpets at my feet that grow,
Are gentle bluebells ringing low.

The choir that sings on wings of song,
Are birds that lead the heavenly throng,
My heart joins in and sings in key,
At what my God's revealed to me.

Julia Salter

THE WILDFOWLER

As the sun sets in the western sky
The fowlers come all full of joy
Will it be their lucky night? One does think as they scale the dykes
And struggle in the mud, sometimes wader high.

They take their positions along the wall
All patiently wait for the wicker of wings
As darkness falls upon the marsh,
One can hear the cries of curlew, redshank, dunlin, too
As they feed on the mud, way out of view.

By now the moon has climbed way up
Lighting the way for the oncoming duck
Quick reflexes a left and right,
I've bagged the first duck of the night,
And as my dog goes out of view,
I think of the sensation one goes through
Shooting on the marsh at night, it's paradise I know
I was one of those fowlers.

C Prentice

CELEBRATE

Let's give ourselves a common toast
And realise what matters most
For in us all there lies a flower
Of brilliance and enormous power
It only takes the will to care
To show us all it is there.

Brenda Roberts

MY PET COELACANTH

My coelacanth, if truth be told, isn't quite a pet,
In fact I must be honest: We haven't even met.

It freely floats and shyly swims in an Indian Ocean trench,
But I've given it some cash support whilst feeling very French:
In the Musee D'Histoire Naturelle in Centre Ville Toulouse
I sponsored my own coelacanth as a conservation ruse.

Ancient fish, once thought extinct, almost older than creation,
Still gulping air, as once did too, your amphibious relation
Who crawled on fingered fins, emerging from primeval ocean,
So many million years ago, on some unexplained emotion.

I know your lifestyle very well through a video display;
Your stuffed and scaly cousin lay, encased along the way.
So few you are, and rarely seen, in your swampy habitat;
I hope my ticket money helps to keep you nice and fat.

And though we may not ever meet, you'll hardly find me frowning,
For if we did, I might well be preoccupied with drowning.
If the fin was on the other foot, a less distressing fate:
My coelacanth, in curry sauce, a Dansak on my plate.

M J Cooper

YOU

I don't know what it is
It must be your smile
For you make me feel so good
And I haven't felt that for a while

You're sincere in what you say
You're sincere in what you do
I suppose that is the reason
Why I fell in love with you

I don't know what's ahead of us
But I hope us is what we'll be
For it's a long time since someone's cared
The way you do for me

This poem isn't up to much
It's to thank you for your care
So remember I'll never hurt you
And for you I'm always there

Aileen Guy

THE GARDEN AT NIGHT

In the black of the night when everyone's asleep
Out of my bed to the garden I creep
Down to the mist of the magical lawn
I can just hear the sound of the flowers yawn

The trees seem sleepy, the leaves waving from
        side to side
Along with the sound of the water, the tide
The differences of the garden from night to day
So much more the plants have to say

Each with a different musical sound
Wailing, sailing, but still on the ground
It seems like they're floating in the air
With their petal-like dresses dancing at a
        flower parade fair

Back to my bedroom I tiptoe and sneak
But somehow I can't seem to sleep
Thinking of the flowers' wonderful choir
The noise seems to get higher and higher

It's not really true, it cannot be
Everything's fading, I cannot see
Is it in my dreams
Or is it as it really seems?

Nicola Jane Baker (10)

A COMA OR FULL STOP?

When the choice is no choice at all
and the sign asks the horse to shut the stable door
when the lights are on but the only people home
are the fairies in the attic of the body all alone

But if you pull the plug
and the light therein goes out
your ears may not deceive you
when you hear hope's silent shout

John Mason

SHINING DIAMOND

The clear cool crystal
Sang as he sat down.
His looks were stony,
His heart and mind
As squashed strawberries,
Ruby red.
His eyes were emeralds,
Cold green pools,
His personality was as water
Shiny, clear, transparent,
Shining diamond.
However hard you looked
You could not see
Its exact colour and form.
But then I found the key
That set him loose.
He was really as natural as
The sand that moves
Washed by the sea,
The sun that glows,
The moon that moves the sea.
And all of this moved by me.

Alison Crawford-Ward

CHELTENHAM PROMENADE

We strolled along the promenade
In the lazy sunshine,
Gazing at the windows of the shops.

Laura Ashley, Windsmoor, Liberty
With gossamer shawls and silks
And a feeling of well being.

She came towards us,
Well dressed and shouting obscenities
Which froze upon the air.

'Did she say that, or that?
With all these visitors here
Whatever will they think!'

She passed us by
With an agonised look,
While we tried not to feel put out.

The sun still shone,
It was Blazers, Gap and Habitat,
And we were glad that she was gone.

Tudor Williams

UNTITLED

That window, I've sat and looked from that window
I've looked on and learned
I've seen seasons come and pass, bright colours come and fade
Orange furnace, burning red and emerald jade.

That window, it's taught me much of things wild and free
I've seen birds swoop, trees grow, animals that are tearaways
The way I'd like to be.

Through it I've watched, like the window of my mind, the food of my soul
A picture of life. I've seen the sky big and bright, full of tight
Birds gifted with beautiful flight.

That window, like a doorway to the sky,
It's bright and gleaming shine reflects the tenderness
Of the blue sky's slow and gentle caress
Of clouds, soft and inviting like marshmallow on a blueberry pie.

That window, a bar between the whispering wind and I
The trees, the fields, they reap the wild winds
Taming and controlling the fierce currents of turmoil.

That window, I watch intensely as the bows sway
The leaves flow in continuous rhapsody
Shredding from bark to ground.
Leaving bare shells of time, but not empty.

That window, it also has seen. It's seen me grow from young to old
Good health to illness, fresh to decay
It shows me the blooming sprays of magnificent arrays
Dressage of living cases enfold a record of years, past, present and
Future.

It has seen the husky voice of winter, smooth voice of summer
The autumn sensuous. It's watched as I have. We've watched dawn arise in
A splendid dawning of pleasure and seen dusk steal down silently but
Surely over precious lands of centuries.

That window, now it watches me, I've outlived my use long ago. The Window has survived it's purpose and looks on knowingly as I slip away Silently, farewell dear friend for I must go.

Amanda Clarke

TWO RIVERS

You and I have been us
    By water, by seas, lakes
And rivers. but mostly rivers.
    Where we have walked and talked
And not been strangers.
    We let the trees drop curtains on the roles we play
For just an hour, a minute or a day,
    It has been you and I - not they.

You say 'Where does it come from
    All this water?' Ceaseless giving -
Like love?
    This wheel revolving binds
The earth and sky
    Always with its circuit through the sea
The wheel will turn for you, for me

But sometime every river finds the sea
    Receiving, giving, hiding, seeking,
Growing old
    Two rivers bound by a loving wheel
The peaceful Dove and blessings Manifold

Megan Hostler

IN THE EYE OF THE BEHOLDER

Such a lovely lady,
Gentle and refined.
Softly spoken, talented,
Nature had been kind.

Until the spell was broken,
When illness overwhelmed.
But even then, could raise a smile,
To all her many friends.

It made you feel so humble,
To see her eyes resigned.
Not a hint of hurt or anger,
To those she would leave behind.

So rest in peace dear friend,
You've truly left your mark.
For all of us to remember,
Your kind, unselfish heart.

J L Dodson

CONFUSION GONE

Thoughts spin, they knot the mind
Why me, what happened?
Something long ago, was I born this way?
When did I realise?
Despair deepens with each question.
What am I doing here, why did I come?
Yet somehow it feels right.
People surround me, all different.
And yet the same.
I want to run and hide
But something holds me to the stool.
I try and shrink into the corner
Move and I'll be noticed.
A voice is raised above the noise,
Someone sits besides me.
Blind panic grips, must get out.
Again the voice breaks through.
'First time, nervous. On your own?'
I turn and look a smile greets my stare.
The panic fades I feel at ease.
A hand pulls me.
Swallowed up among the throng of people
The dancefloor takes us on.
Inch by inch the closeness draws
Still unsure yet certain.
This is right. This is me. No more denial.
A moments hesitation, four hands combine.
Confusion gone, I'm certain now
New life, new friends, first love.

Rick Lansbury

PSSST!

Got a secret? Why keep it?
Get real, what's the deal?
Tight lipped, mouth zipped
Unrevealing, no one squealing
Keeping mum, acting dumb
Huggermugger, stubborn bugger
Hiding matters, minding manners
Special agent sly, why so shy?
Lack of talk makes me balk
Don't be cute, mute, shoot!
Speak geek, let it leek
I'll lend an ear, I've got to hear
Deliberate, contemplate, speculate, enunciate,
Articulate, intimate, communicate, illuminate.
At your command I'll understand
At your voice I'll rejoice
To your oration my adoration.
Remove the screens, spill the beans
Unzip, let slip, gossip
Rumour, rancour, cut to candour.
Be a flirt, dish the dirt
Be a dear, start a smear
Be a guy, live a lie
Tell your brothers, tell your sisters
Give the others Chinese whispers.
In the end we'll still be friends
For you and I, we've got it sussed
With heads held high, in God we trust.

Graeme Craig

FREEDOM OF MIND

A moment to think is the birth of inspiration,
Close your eyes and dream its freedom of the mind,
Playing holds the key to inexhaustible youth,
A laugh a day is music of the soul,
Smile and share your happiness,
Be ready to talk there is someone waiting to listen,
Take time to listen you might miss a beautiful word,
Learn how to share, life is too short to be selfish,
Look after the people you love and they will respond,
Love and be loved, a perfect creation.

Amanda Whitehead

TOMORROW

Like

        our   emotions

             the

words

        tumbled and

               tripped.

Following   us

             down

        through

             the

               years.

David Blair

GROWING UP

Only parents know the joys that children bring
and the heartaches
When they soar away on wings
of independent spirits

Pausing to reflect on times gone by
and how my parents worried
Why
could I not see then what I see now?
Immaturity of youth? A stubborn streak?
Parents, listen, let your children speak . . .

Patience brings knowledge
and hopes abound
When you see your children have found
in themselves
Your maturity.

Monica Watson

RADIO ALARM

Up in the morning,
Its tune blaring out.
My head still is stuffy,
I'm up and about.
The constant voices,
The prying glare.
Shouting 'Good morning!'
It seems so unfair.
In my sleeping refuge,
My duvet, I lay.
Turn it off. Back to sleep?
It's the start of the day.
So open the curtains,
Let in the light.
It's far too early -
To be saying goodnight.

Sarah Lucy Dunkley

A COLLECTION OF WORDS

Communicating much!
On subjects - various -
Needed to touch
The minds of people
Everywhere in the world
Man's spiritual reflections
Prompted by inner thoughts
Outpouring on paper
Recollections with connections
Adding speculative suggestions
Reading and reciting
Yielding sentences

Passed on via speech
Or an attempt to reach
Eye, if not ear - nonetheless -
Meticulously achieving poetic success!

D A Crawford

A WAY WITH WORDS

Here I sit
Inspired with his every word
Taking in everything that he had to say.
To me and to everyone
To all of us there present.

A way with words

That's what he had.
Full of knowledge
Full of confidence.
Full of laughter.

It was today, the first of March
A new day a new month.
A new experience
A new inspiration, full of magical
gifts.
That what he had a very
special gift,
That shown through his speech,
and every word he spoke.

Lisa French

ROOTS

Together we are like a tree
So stable and so firm
Sometimes I'll branch out on my own
But you know I will return

Often I will shed my leaves
I cover a lot of ground
And then it's back to you I come
To where true love can be found

Sometimes we will germinate
And create saplin's from new shoots
But no matter how far my branches go
I'll always come back to my roots

Maybe sometimes I do stray too far
Trying to sow my seeds
And I know if I'm not careful
I'll get smothered by the weeds

But I think I know my limits
And just how far to go
Because after all is said and done
There's only so many seeds to sow

And when I've finished growing wild
My leaves now withered and brown
It's back to my roots I go again
Maybe this time I'll settle down.

Linda Troop

THE PEEPING ANGEL

Sitting, standing, kneeling, in the morning
Stretching through the coloured glass
In the evening sombre and sedate
Every second day in the holy house
The cavernous high-ceilinged house
Have I been centred intently
By a still and stony gaze
But sat I unobserved with panoramic eyes
That failed to catch my keeper
Steady staring all the while
From amongst select and sacred lives

Until one morning leaf-torn and damp
I sauntered down the aisle uneasy
Took my place as a holy impostor
And babbled in English and Irish whispers
Then sat up and waited the priest
My eyes lifting and sweeping
I am taking this house to my grave

Just then I spied a holy face
Frozen by the sculptor
Looking out from the wall
Fixing upon me over the altar
A gentle blessed face within shadows
Cast cruel and unfair without thought
A face gathered with others as pure
Each seeking a patron for glances
Between pillar, priest and candle
Sought I refuge to find it and more
An open door and the eyes of an angel
That sees me out of the dark
Awaits me under the long windows
And cedes me the beauty of sight
I have nothing but sweet days
Warm winters ahead.

Máirtín Ó Catháin

125

JUST YOU

Count the flowers, you will find,
The years that God has been so kind,
To put such as you on this earth,
When gold is the only thing of worth,
The only thing more so, it's true,
You are the one I love, just you.

J A Kerr

ENCHANTED FOREST

In the mirror of my eye
Parrots blue, go flying by
There before my startled gaze
In a forest, green as jade
Elephants, as big as uncle,
Drowse the magic hours away.
Saying now to one another
'Buns again for tea today.'

Hippos, big as granny, mutter
I'm too old for bread and butter
And with shouts of loud derision
Jump into the mud with glee,
Saying, 'Last one in's a soppy'
Look out chaps - it won't be me.

Tigers, laying in the sun
Paint their stripes on, one by one.
Saying, with a roar, 'My dear
Mind the paint behind my ear!'

Lions, lording by the river
Curl their manes to look quite smart,
Saying now to one another,
'Let's go home before it's dark.'

You, of course, may not believe me
Say these things could never be,
But, my dears, I see them plainly
And you could - if you were me.

S C Preston

HORMONES (HORMOANS!)

It's just my hormones playing tricks on me again,
I hate everything around me, especially men!
I try to keep control of it, but my emotions start to churn,
There's just no making sense of it, why do I feel so stern!

Every molehill seems a mountain, every spot a full blown boil,
Everything seems so much blacker, every tiny chore such toil!

'Can't you see your shoes are dirty? Don't you talk to me that way!
Do you have to get so shirty! Now why can't you see my way?'

The desire for chocolate seizes me and firmly takes a hold,
I've got Mars bars in the cupboard. Cadbury's Dairy Milk ice cold,
I've got double choc chip cookies which I hide away from view
And whenever I am passing I will snaffle one or two!

I feel tired, jaded, listless and a whiter shade of pale,
Every simple task is hopeless every project doomed to fail!

My face is drawn my eyes are red, I crumple into tears!
And all those little problems now become my greatest fears!

My speech is slurred, my memory lost, the list's too long to mention!
What is this thing that plagues me, yes you've guessed . . .
         - Pre-menstrual tension! -

Beverley Squires

INTRO

I start off life amidst such a frenzy,
Squashed, then brightness and someone slaps me.
Lots of big people with smiling faces,
An expectant father who no longer paces.
With body unbunched I'm glad to be free,
There's a cry in the air and it happens to be me.
Time for a nap, although I've just been born,
My first comment on life is a great big yawn.

Tim Challis

CHOCOLATE

In the beginning a thought, half-formed, awareness
Contemplate it, follow, it, ensnare the dream.
Yes, a desire now, and growing stronger
A longing, an obsession, filling all senses.
Abandon rational thought, the desire is king.

In the act a greed, self-centred instinct
Want it, get it, have it, it will be mine.
Chemicals to the brain, senses overload
Inhale the scent, explore the taste, texture lingers.
Give in to sensory rule, the experience is all.

In the afterglow fulfilment, relief, warm content
Breathe it, revel in it, bathe in the light.
Released now and growing calmer, calm.
Rational once more, a comfort, a pleasant moment passed
Don't grieve for it now, there will be others.

In the end guilt, shame, a regret for self-image lost
Stickiness clings, thirst rises, then desire again.
Lack of willpower gave rise to a momentary lapse of control.
A longing, an obsession filling all senses.
Abandon rational thought, the desire is king.

Jan Eyton

LETTING GO

Letting go is part of love,
Perhaps the hardest thing to do,
To know what's best and what is right,
And to *let go*.

To watch your children as they grow,
And go out into their world,
To feel their pride, and share their joy,
And to *let go*.

To want to care, and just *be there*,
To want to be the centre,
Of someone else's world's unfair,
You must *let go*.

I loved you deeply, and still do,
In fact, it never lessens,
But more and more I am aware,
I must *let go*.

But bonds of love that tie us all,
Are very very strong,
Though they may stretch, they do not break,
I can't *let go*.

Evelyn Arslan

THE CITY

I feel disheartened when the music roars.
Yet I feel comforted because of the opening doors.
My tongue is pulled out and my eyes opened wide.
My life is at war with the buildings at my side.
Through the mist, comes a monster from the deep,
To disturb my pleasant, restful sleep.
The offices begin to rise from the depths of slumber.
People walk around, increasing in number.
The day has begun and it brings lots of fun.
They stand under me, a shade from the sun.
Like ants they flock away, for their meals in dens.
And return like a group of squawking hens.
I see a beggar with a worn out copper tin,
He looks so weak and horrendously thin.
The shops begin to close, go away with the wind.
While the street lights up, the noise has dimmed.
A push and a tug and in goes my tongue,
It was if I had done something terribly wrong.
A murky mist falls over the city.
Till tomorrow when we rise, oh what a pity!

Louisa J Shilton (11)

LOVE IS BORN

I don't understand the effect you have on me
It is alien
You have touched my heart and taken something
It hurts

How can this be so
What is time
When I cannot remember not knowing you
Like a baby arriving

Have we met somewhere before
In another time
For me to feel so completely close to you
Perhaps we are soul mates

The purity of the love I feel for you
Cannot be wrong
It stems from deep within my being
All it craves is your nourishment

Catherine McAuley

THE FORGOTTEN KING

Not knowing where you come from,
Nor the colours you adorn,
Can lead to false conclusion
And misinterpreted aims,
Not to mention a yearning for recognition.

Well concealed behind dark glasses,
The story in your eyes,
Those calm and jewelled pools of mourning
That long for afternoon,
They shall retire until the weekend comes around.

I sink down into my dream chair,
That sponge filled, artificial resting place
Where I can escape from the problems of survival
And nestle in the arms
Of a long wished for fantasy.

Back in the real world problems abound,
I feel the abhorred presence
Of misery and grief,
Giggling like school girls as they prod my mind
And torment me with thoughts of heaven.

How can I lose this rancid conscience,
A fevered mind is all I own,
Casting sharp images of terrible occurrences
Into my dreams and wishful thoughts,
Where I can't even rule my own realms.

Paul Davidson

THE APPOINTMENT

Alone I waited
but the clock ticked on.

Gusting wind
and sheeting rain
sealed the house
and me within
my warm cocoon,
but the clock ticked on.

Last year's roses'
hip tipped fingers
startled the glass
and my taught nerves,
but the clock ticked on.

Wellington boots,
musty smelling,
and mackintosh,
cold as death;
as I emerged
into the rain
my time had come -
but the clock ticked on.

Pat Rollnick

THE OTHER SIDE

Up they rose, the phantoms in the night
To dance from their lairs and begin shift of fright
Flitting from stones and trees to torment living kind
To add to their number, no conscience to mind

From all corners of the dark, they do come to mischief
Many past hauntings, like poppies on a wreath
Tormenting people and place, where they last breathed life
Bringing with them woe, as well as trouble and strife

Many are famed but all are bound
Secrets of the afterlife, they can utter no sound
Moaning and wailing, dragging chain and holding head
Each has a burden, only known to the dead

Our night is their day and our day their night
When light breaks through - end of shift, out of sight
We will find out one day, of the things they know and hold
For reasons of hauntings we will be told

Their nightshift in summer is short, freedom not long
Winter is a lengthy blackness, when their power is strong
Asking questions of the other side, in this life shouldn't be
Known
We will soon understand and know, when our life is outgrown.

Paul Muir

GARTH

The height of summer
It's a glorious day,
This town is a prison
I must get away.

I'll go for a stroll
To somewhere I've been,
A magical place
So peaceful, serene.

I close my door
To return to the wild,
I crave for the freedom
I knew as a child.

I'm getting so close now
To my wonderful dream,
Where the plants and the animals
Work as a team.

I remember this place
Those houses weren't there,
They are breaking and stabbing
I wasn't aware.

They are hurting the mountain
For monetary gain,
But the mountain is screaming
They are causing it pain.

The sky is so dark now
It's going to cry,
They have broken Garth's heart
It is going to die.

To all who have been there
You will understand why,
I must try to save it
I can't say good-bye.

Lisa Geen

CLOUDS

On Monday a battleship passed by,
Slowly, quietly, with great majesty,
Treating all around with pure disdain.

On Tuesday a shoal of fish came into view,
Hardly moving, yet never touching,
And silent.

Wednesday wore a myriad of colours,
Blues and greys, ever changing from
Second to second.

Thursday was loud, and rushing by,
Fleeing from the dark pursuer.

Friday saw God's promise to Noah,
In seven hues so gloriously made
for all to see.

Saturday brought the tortoise, and the hare,
One slowly ambling along,
The other swiftly, dreaming away.

On Sunday all was blue, and quiet.
The clouds had gone.
They too needed a day of rest.

Sandra Nicholas

FOREVER COMPLETELY

Gently, gently,
Softly, softly,
Warm and slowly
Come and hold me.

Love me, lead me
Herd me, weed me
Show your flowing fruitful wonders.

Listen, teach me,
Rush to reach me,
Bring your ear of passioned kindness.
Bond your timeless heart to mine.

Veronica Cooke

STARS

Pinhole stars sparkle
through their dark screen,
a flowing vision cascading
from a long forgotten dream.

The scales on tiny fish
in shoals of a deep pool,
darting through space
thousands in their school.

Lovers Orion and Sirius
together as legend said,
are settling now as spawn
upon a gravely redd.

Damien Mallon

TO SEARCH FOR APHRODITE

Go now, go down to yonder sea.
Gentle maiden, wild beast.
Seek her out, seek her there.
She waits for thee on milk white surf.
Softly lapping to and fro
To draw thee in, send thee back.
You'll find her in the salty air.

Look now, look out at yonder moon.
Gentle radiance, powerful madness.
Seek her out, seek her there.
She waits for thee in silvery light.
Softly pulling to and fro
To take thee out, bring thee back.
Embrace her sensual midnight glare.

Reach now, reach out for unseen lands.
Gentle lover, astral queen.
Seek her out, seek her there.
In woven threads of magic realm.
Softly ebbing to and fro
To pull thee up, bring thee down.
Behold her golden kingdom fair.

Ashley Jones

ANOTHER ANNUNCIATION

Arcing down the sky she came,
Her ports all flaring red,
The long, cold way from Ceti III
Yet all her crew lay dead,

They watched her as she scored the sky
Her motors running sweet,
Regina Coeli had returned
And most hearts missed a beat.

She settled light as thistledown
And stood so gleaming still
Among the red-stained holly trees
Beneath a holy hill.

Who brought her in? Who set her down?
Who rode the jets that night?
They discovered from the skipper's log
Englowed in unearthly light.

In characters of red and gold
The story still they tell,
Of a tragedy in far out space
Logged up by Gabriel.

R F Hamilton

RESPITE

Two weeks in limbo . . .
Strange faces, requiring not my presence,
Indifferent to my being,
Release me from effort.

Slowly, as mind and body unwinds
To slow tempo, inertia assails me.
That other life seems distant,
Vague to think upon.

Yet, lurking behind the inertia,
Veiled in the limbo,
I know the time will come
To surface and recoil the spring.

The peaceful sky and rhythmic waves
Wash my brain.
Timeless they are.
For a short spell, we are as one.

But I know, certain as the tide,
My time to turn is near;
To swell to life and purpose
And cease to drift.

And, when living goes too fast,
With pressures all demanding,
Within, I shall draw upon the peace
From limbo, sky and waves and find release.

Pauline Boncey

PANDORA

I have traced the heavens I dare not wait
The lines converge to seal man's fate,
        I must find your box Pandora
I send my mind into the breeze
To search the earth the seven seas,
        I seek your box Pandora
I leap through time to fabled places
See the secret of the long lost races,
        I know your lair Pandora
I glimpse into the pits of hell
Where all the ills of mankind dwell,
        I see your box Pandora
Now the third millennium day draws near
When all mankind must shed its fear,
        I have your box Pandora
From the sacred land of Calvary
I bring the gift of a holy key,
        I have closed your box Pandora
For on that day I shall turn the key
Then cast it to the deepest sea,
        I have locked your box Pandora.

Adsum

145

APOLLO

Apollo met on a subway,
In close communion with the strap.
A shower of sparks litter locks dazzled with grey.

Apollo's sweat is clean as apples
Great clouds of August wheat are threshed in his eyes.
A winter landscape in the hollow of his back.

His hands as cool and nonchalant as willows in winter
His lips like heather and his teeth like ground glass
His breath as sweet and intimate as children's litanies
Beneath his ribs a torment of green grass.

He draws us haltered through fenceless fields of reason
To fallow places long left unfrequented
Ripe fruit fermented in another season

Rose Croghan

Butterfly on a ledge,
With a broken wing.
Such frail beauty,
Such a fickle wind.

Sión Hamilton

FOGBOUND

The lounge is full of people.
Arrivals diverted to other towns.
Departures are all on the ground.
Fogbound.

The forecast says clearer by lunch-time.
Nothing to do, no engine sound.
It seems to be coming down thicker
Fogbound.

Appointments are missed, vacations delayed.
Rumours are passed around.
'The worst for years, will last for days.'
Fogbound.

I'm here in the terminal building.
I'm wishing that you were around,
I'm missing you more than ever.
Fogbound.

John Davis

A PIG'S TALE

Shades of Orwell, long since gone.
Who forecast a thing or two.
His porcine community down on the farm
Never guessed what their progeny would do
Ten years on, we've reached a stage
When piggies don't just live in a sty
But take to the air in cargo planes
And fly.

Round the world goes the British porker
On hoof, but sometimes as bacon
Only of course *the more equal ones*
Those of higher station.

Then there are those who don't go at all
But send their best wishes in semen
Then piglets as far as France and Spain
Or as far as Norway and Sweden
Suddenly find themselves pregnant again
Without even knowing the reason.

Norman E Taylor

TIME TO STAND AND STARE

I was walking alone, it was growing dark
The daylight fast fading away
In a deepening grey sky the moon arose
And it seemed to have something to say
It seemed to tell me 'Look up, look up!'
So I did, and what did I see,
But the beauties of heaven, mid moon and stars
And it seemed they were made just for me
The following morning the sun bade me wake
And on pulling the blinds back I found
That a spider had built me a beautiful web
Which the dawn had with jewels adorned
The sun seemed to tell me 'Go for a walk'
So I did, and all that I saw
In the heavens and earth portrayed wonderful love
And to think that the Lord made it all!
But we rush on and on, and we go to and forth
And scarcely think about prayer,
Or of saying a thank you for all of the joys
Portrayed so lovingly there
The moon and the stars and the milky way,
The flowers, birds, trees, sky and air
And the frost rain and sun, snow and thunder storms too,
Yes the loving Lord God put them there
Each insect and animal, even the pests
Like the ant and the slug and the flea
I thank you Lord God for this wonderful earth
That it seems you have made - just for me!

Dot Holloway

WAIT AND SEE

Now that the first notes of peace
Have travelled here,
Floating in the breeze for every
Northern man to hear:

Who will heal the broken hearts?
Who will rebuild what's been torn
Apart?

Now that the first notes of peace
Have been sung;
Is violence really dead? Has peace
Really won?

From violence shall we forever
Be free?
God only knows - let's wait and see.

Cathy Thomas

INFORMATION

We hope you have enjoyed reading this book - and that you will continue to enjoy it in the coming years.

If you like reading and writing poetry drop us a line, or give us a call, and we'll send you a free information pack.

Write to

Poetry Now Information
1-2 Wainman Road
Woodston
Peterborough
PE2 7BU.